My Prayers

Matthew 18:19 Again I say to you that if two of you agree on earth concerning anything that they ask, it will be done for them by My Father in heaven.

There are moments in your life that have no rhyme or reason, seemingly insignificant, a moment that looks ordinary and then God shows up in ways you would never expect just to show you there is never nothing going on, that every moment is a precious one and some are extraordinary and just waiting for you to show up. That is what happened on Monday, June 8th, 2009 riding from Anadarko to Cordell with a lunch break in Mt. View at the cafeteria where there was an angel among us who's name is Jessica... That day changed my life forever, the day love found me, a beautiful child who loves me with nothing required and inspires me to be a better person, to search for new ways to be a pleasure in the sight of God without expectation of it's return. When I left that day I didn't know Oklahoma FreeWheel chooses a different route every year so you can imagine my disappointment when the next year we didn't go through there and I thought I would never see Jessica again. In August 2012 I was late for a nail appointment and chose to go as a walk in and there was Jessica and even more amazing is she remembered me and I remembered her. From that moment we have remained in touch and make time for each other. Patches, I love you and your family with a gratitude that there are no words for, thank you for welcoming me into your family.

Ask God to OPEN YOUR EYES to see what is already in you (Ephesians 1:18, Ephesians 3:20). The Holy Spirit is in you. The Love of God is in you. Faith is in you. These forces of God's power are in you right now. Affirm this, I am complete in Christ. There is no good thing missing in my life. I have all things in Him. My God supplies all my needs, and I expect His supply TODAY. I have the peace of God, which delivers my heart from trouble and disappointment. Even if people let me down, my God will uphold me and help me. I have the Holy Spirit, the love of God and the gift of faith in my life. I am complete in Him, in Jesus' Name!
To my beautiful family, I come to you today in prayer through the love of Christ, the power of the Holy Ghost, and the authority of God our father that blessing be placed before you and should they be disguised as challenges you are prepared to see the opportunity and embrace it with passion. I pray for the genuine forgiveness that heals any hurts or wrongs. It strengthens the disheartened soul that has lost its way. It refreshes and renews our hope. It is through forgiveness that we are "born again" and "become like a child." In this way we regain the precious attitude of a willing mind that is ready to learn all over again as for me I am just a girl, a child of God who realizes that I fall short of Gods grace everyday and I recognize that God gives it to me out of his amazing grace. I am blessed each day that I awake and choose to share it with all of God's children. Thank you father for blessing me with what I don't deserve and protecting me from what I do deserve. I am enough for God and that's enough for me, I have placed my eyes upon him and found the truth in I pray that you also allow God to soften your soul to forgive completely, give gratitude infinitely and find your eyes upon him because only then will you see… I pray that you see the gifts placed before you, I thank you authentically for coming into my life for a moment in time, for a lifetime, and for eternity. I freely pray for you love, health and wealth in abundance through Gods grace… Amen
~Lisa Christiansen

Isaiah 55:11
11) so is my word that goes out from my mouth:
It will not return to me empty,
but will accomplish what I desire
and achieve the purpose for which I sent it.

Here on the pulse of this new day you may have the grace to look up and out and into your sister's eyes, into your brother's face, your country and say simply, very simply with hope good morning. Ever, did you ever, sit down and wonder about what freedom's freedom would bring? it's so easy to be free you start by loving yourself then those who look like you all else will come naturally... Sometimes the things that may or may not be true are the things you need to believe in the most. That people are basically good; that honor, courage, and virtue mean everything; that power and money, money and power mean nothing; that good always triumphs over evil; and I want you to remember this, that love... true love never dies. You remember that because it doesn't matter if it's true or not. The reason you should believe in those things is because those are the things worth believing in, hope lives in believing and faith is believing in what you cannot see... There is no greater love than God's grace and mercy...

~Lisa Christiansen

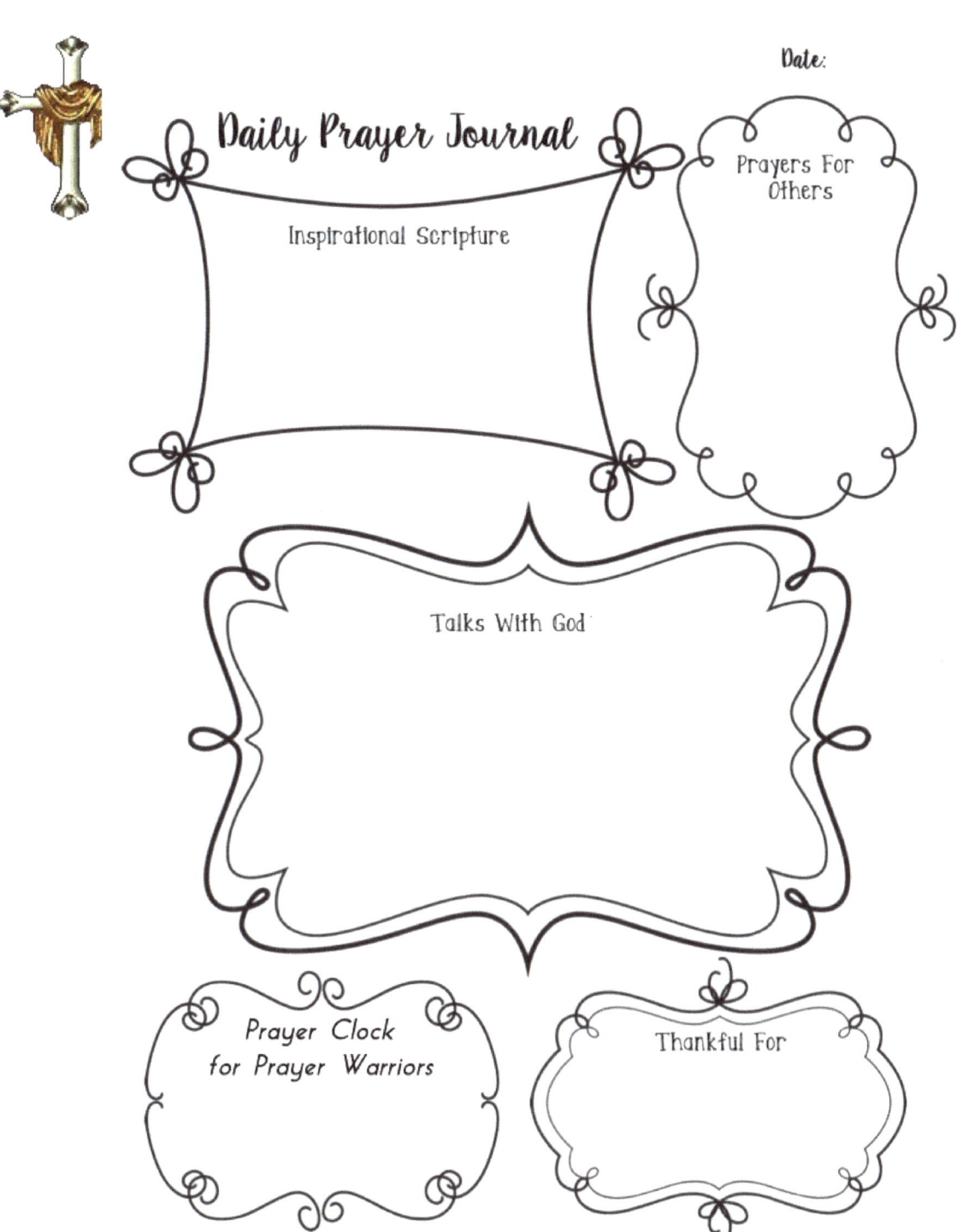

I come to you today in prayer through the love of Christ, the power of the Holy Ghost, and the authority of God our father that blessing be placed before you, I pray for the genuine forgiveness that heals any hurts or wrongs. It strengthens the disheartened soul that has lost its way. It refreshes and renews our hope. It is through forgiveness that we are "born again" and "become like a child." In this way we regain the precious attitude of a willing mind that is ready to learn all over again as for me I am just a girl, a child of God who realizes that I fall short of Gods grace everyday and I recognize that God gives it to me out of his amazing grace. I pray for the lost to find their way and for God's mercy to rest upon those that have passed without accepting Christ for their salvation that they may be spared and given a home in heaven even if it means my soul must take their place. Amen

~Lisa Christiansen

Isaiah 55:11
11) so is my word that goes out from my mouth:
It will not return to me empty,
but will accomplish what I desire
and achieve the purpose for which I sent it.

Isaiah 11:6
6) "The wolf also shall dwell with the lamb,
The leopard shall lie down with the young goat,
The calf and the young lion and the fatling together;
And a little child shall lead them.

Father in heaven my heart is humbled by your amazing grace that you smile upon me each day. Everyday I wake humbled in gratitude for the blessings I could never earn or deserve and for your infinite willingness to protect me from what I do deserve. There are no words to express the depth, breadth or width of my gratitude for these daily actions that you choose to abundantly with generous proportion bless me with, it is my honor to confess with my mouth and every fiber of my earthly vessel that you Lord are my God, my savior and my purpose for being; for as long as I have breath and for as long as I live I will sing your praise, share your word and be filled so completely with you God that others will desire to know you and those that don't believe will question their disbelief. Father, thank you for your faithfulness, your commitment, and your sacrificing your only son Jesus Christ to shed his blood of redemption through our veins that we may live life and live it more abundantly in gratitude. Father thank you for welcoming the souls who have passed without accepting your son Jesus Christ even if this means I must take their place that they may live in your mercy and grace in your bountiful kingdom. Thank you for that when I speak it is you they hear, when others see me they see you, father thank you for another day to testify to your greatness. I love you and I will stand even if this means I must stand alone. I have infinite trust, I will forever walk by faith and I have unshakable belief. With the power of the Holy Ghost through the everlasting love of Jesus Christ, embraced in your grace. Amen.

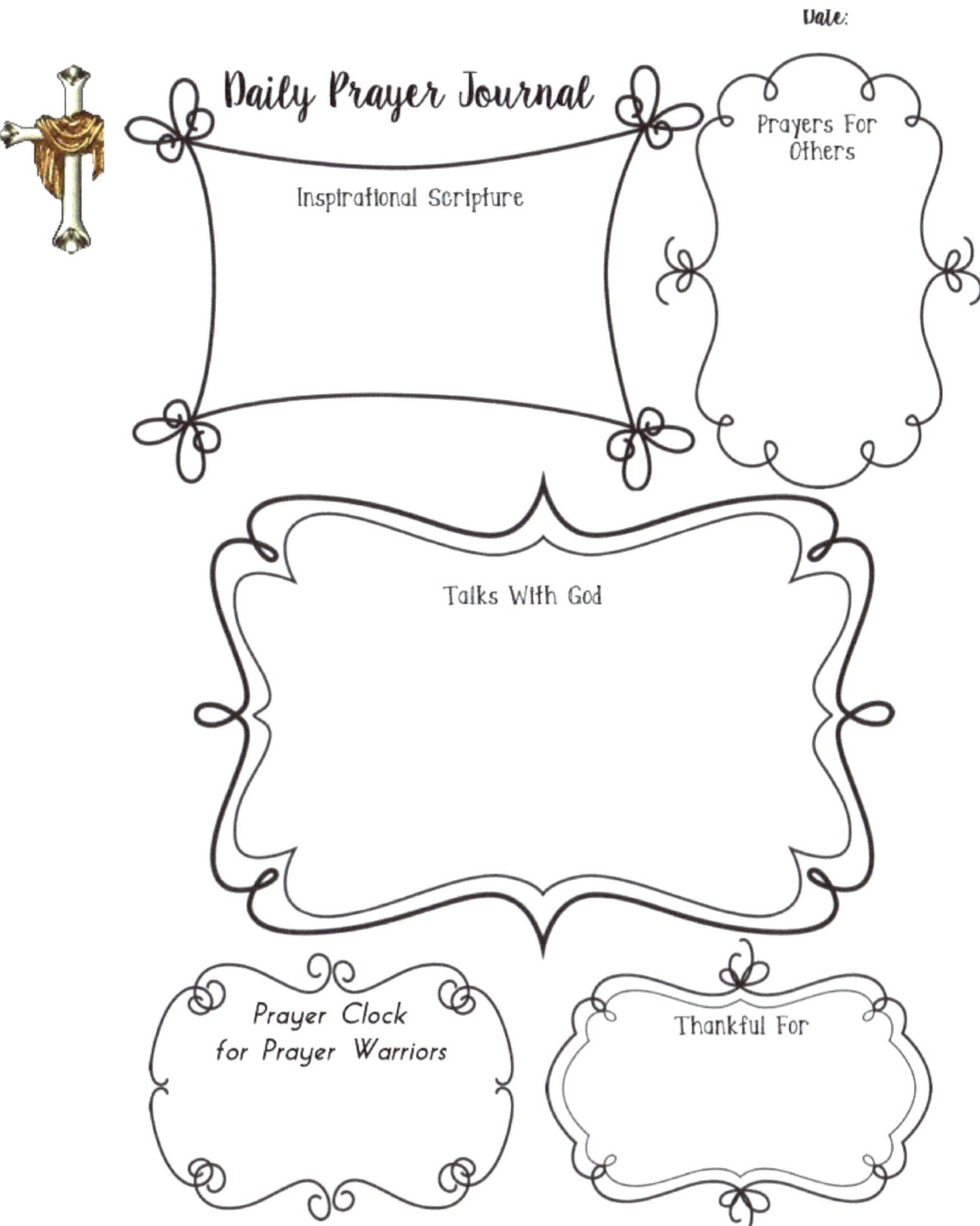

Have you ever had a moment of overwhelming gratitude that there are simply no words? Yesterday was a moment of silent exhilaration and appreciation of God's amazing grace, a wave of oceans flooding me with humble gratitude brought me to my knees and in this moment I continue to feel God's faithfulness. I will forever be his servant to testify to his greatness in every moment, this is amazing grace filled with unfailing love. Father God thank you for your servant son Jesus Christ, Lord of Lord's, King of Kings, my Savior my God to whom I come before on bended knee in humble gratitude to praise your Holy name on high. I am speechless for every blessing you have brought into my life and continue to bring to me, thank you for the abundant blessings, the opportunities and the vision to recognize even the intangible gifts you continue to bless me with. Father God I love you most faithfully, with a refreshed and renewed fervent passion from my reborn heart, thank you for the gift of seeing this world through the eyes of a child, for loving others through the soul with the innocence of a child and the heart to live in faith with the trust of an infant. Father thank you for everything, for the things unseen, unheard, and intangible because I recognize it's not what you see it's what you don't see that grows beyond measure, thank you for giving me life. I recognize everyday is a gift and as I awake each morning I choose to share it with all of God's children with the intention to touch one heart, to move one soul, to inspire one life. Thank you father as you continue to stand before me, beside me and within me. In Jesus Holy name through the power of the Holy Ghost, embraced in your everlasting love. Amen.

Father in heaven above as I look up I see your face, I stand tallest kneeled before you in my humble gratitude of the blessings you continue to place before me each and everyday in abundant proportion far exceeding my expectations and father because of your strength I stand even when I stand alone, because of your grace I am saved and thrive in the warmth of your embrace, because of your mercy I forgive the inexcusable because you have forgiven the inexcusable in each of us, and father I pray to touch one heart with your love, to move one soul with your mercy, and to inspire one life with your grace. Father I am faithfully yours, I am grateful for my life, for the gift of living my life through the eyes of a child while trusting everyone with the innocence of an infant in the arms of sweet amazing grace. Father thank you for sacrificing your sweet son Jesus Christ to shed his powerful blood of redemption through our veins that we may live in absolute gratitude and have everlasting life. Amen.
~Lisa

Ephesians 2: 8-10
8 For it is by grace you have been saved, through faith and this is not from yourselves, it is the gift of God 9 not by works, so that no one can boast. 10 For we are God's handiwork, created in Christ Jesus to do good works, which God prepared in advance for us to do.

My God I come before you on bended knee in front of the world to see me in my humble gratitude completely vulnerable in my infinite weakness to expose my soul for you to enter into with your infinite, perfect strength to speak that others may hear you in my words and see you in my actions. Thank you for opening doors that no man can shut and blessing me beyond what I could ever earn or deserve, thank you for always completely protecting me in your shelter of amazing grace and mercy from what I absolutely do deserve for I was born into this world with sin and through your grace you sacrificed your only son on the cross to shed his innocent blood of absolution and redemption to flow through each of our veins that we may live in absolute gratitude because of your forgiveness. Father each day I awake I choose to search for new ways to be a blessing in your eyes that you may smile your grace upon my face that your light may shine from within my soul to soften my heart for your love to live, thank you for breaking through the chains of bondage of each of us that we may all breakthrough to the innocence of a child that we may live from the child within each of us because it is only then that we may enter your kingdom and father I pray gratitude in advance for the forgiveness of those who have passed without accepting your son Jesus Christ as their Lord and Savior even if this means I must take their place because I cannot think of any greater act of love than to take their place that they may receive your grace and see your mercy in your kingdom for I have been selfish in my youth and this is the one thing I can do to say thank you for the abundant blessings you continue to place before me and within me; father I offer a selfless act as I stand even if this means I stand alone, father I have no idea what I have done to receive such grace and abundance of mercy and blessings and for this reason I am committed to search for new ways everyday to continue to be a pleasure in your sight. I love you, I have faith and I believe. In Jesus most Holy name. Amen.

~Lisa Christiansen

Daily Prayer Journal

Date:

Inspirational Scripture

Prayers For Others

Talks With God

Prayer Clock for Prayer Warriors

Thankful For

Father I come before you tonight with a joyous heart filled with the faith of a child and with the trust of an infant. Thank you Father for blessing me with each passing moment beyond measure in abundant proportion, truly I am humbled in my gratitude as I come before you on bended knee standing taller than ever as I kneel before you in immeasurable gratitude for your amazing grace and mercy as you flood my soul with your faithful and unfailing love. Father thank you for standing beside me, before me and within me to use my weakness as your strength. Thank you for the gift of seeing this world through the eyes of a child, thank you for the gift of a heart of a child with blind trust to believe see the best in everyone, thank you for the opportunities placed before me each day and the ability to recognize the opportunity to be a blessing to others, father I am grateful and honored to sing your praises each day because for as long as I have breath and as long as I have life I commit to singing your praise, sharing your word and living in gratitude. Thank you father for sacrificing your son Jesus Christ to shed his innocent blood of absolution for our redemption to flood through our veins to wash away our sins that we may always remember to live in gratitude for the forgiveness you have given us through your amazing grace and mercy. Father thank you for blessing those who have passed without accepting Jesus christ with your forgiveness that they may experience your kingdom even if this means I must take their place, I will stand even if this means I stand alone because I know I have been born into sin and I was selfish in my youth, there are not words to express me gratitude for your blessing me with more than I could ever earn or deserve and you continue protect me beyond what I could earn or deserve and for this I can show you through my actions by standing tall kneeled before you always. I love you father, I have faith, trust, and I believe in your faithful unfailing love. I say mountain move and so it is done. Amen.

Isaiah 55:11 so is my word that goes out from my mouth: It will not return to me empty, but will accomplish what I desire and achieve the purpose for which I sent it.

Father God in heaven above I come before you on bended knee humbled before you with gratitude beyond measure for the debt you paid through sacrificing your son Jesus Christ to shed his innocent blood of absolution and forgiveness that we may have everlasting life and have it more abundantly, this is a debt I could never earn, deserve or repay. I am just a girl, a child of God who is here only by God's grace and mercy against all odds and only because God continues to hold me in the palm of his hand for a purpose beyond my understanding and I am living on purpose in the present recognizing the fruitful blessings placed before me, beside me and with me in abundant proportion through the grace of God as he stands before me, beside me and within me through the power of the Holy Ghost with the everlasting love of Jesus Christ while embraced in his mercy to dress me in the whole armor of God. I am here to sing his praises for as long as I have breath and for as long as I have life I will share his word and I will forever kneel before my Lord and Savior Jesus Christ because I recognize this is the only time I stand tallest and I will forever be his vessel to share his word through my every action and through every word that when I speak others will hear my God and through my actions they will see his blessings as I search for new ways to be a blessing in the sight of God everyday, I am filled with a joyous heart and a soul filled with peace because of my gratitude for the immeasurable abundance of God continuing to bless me beyond my needs that I may continue to give beyond my means with the faith of a child as I live through the soul of an infant to see the world through the eyes of our Lord and Savior, our sweet Jesus Christ because I will forever commit and rededicate to always live by example rather than lead by ignorance. Father Thank you in advance for accepting those who have not accepted Christ into your most glorious kingdom that they may experience your grace and mercy even if this means I must take their place because I too was born into sin and have been selfish in my youth and while I can't change the past I can live by example in my every action. Father thank you for always protecting me from what I most certainly do deserve and for blessing me with what I could never earn or deserve. Father with every breath I confess with my mouth out loud that Jesus Christ is and forever is my Lord and Savior, father I pray all of these things in Jesus most Holy name, I have faith, trust and I believe. Amen.
~Lisa Christiansen

Father in heaven above as I look up I see your face, I stand tallest kneeled before you in my humble gratitude of the blessings you continue to place before me each and everyday in abundant proportion far exceeding my expectations and father because of your strength I stand even when I stand alone, because of your grace I am saved and thrive in the warmth of your embrace, because of your mercy I forgive the inexcusable because you have forgiven the inexcusable in each of us, and father I pray through my actions and my voice to touch one heart with your love, to move one soul with your mercy, and to inspire one life with your grace. Father I am faithfully yours, I am grateful for my life, for the gift of living my life through the eyes of a child while trusting everyone with the innocence of an infant in the arms of sweet amazing grace. Father thank you for sacrificing your sweet son Jesus Christ to shed his powerful blood of redemption through our veins that we may live in absolute gratitude and have everlasting life, I have faith, trust, and I believe with everything that is me in you. Amen.
~Lisa Christiansen
Ephesians 2: 8-10
8 For it is by grace you have been saved, through faith and this is not from yourselves, it is the gift of God 9 not by works, so that no one can boast. 10 For we are God's handiwork, created in Christ Jesus to do good works, which God prepared in advance for us to do.

Daily Prayer Journal

Date:

Inspirational Scripture

Prayers For Others

Talks With God

Prayer Clock for Prayer Warriors

Thankful For

On this beautiful day I am reminded how abundantly blessed I am in generous proportion beyond expectation, I am humbled in my honor to call each of you "family" and I absolutely LOVE each of YOU. I am overwhelmed in my gratitude of the clear providence of God's gifts in each of you and because of each of you I am reminded today that nothing else matters beyond God's grace, I was born fighting my way into this world and against all odds God had other plans and today I am here only by God's grace and I choose to make a stand to share God's word with every breath I take, with every beat of my heart, on every platform I am offered. I am a child of God and while I may not know what tomorrow holds I do know who holds my future and because of my God I am unshakable, with passion, and most of all with love, the most pure love from the child within me that God has instructed me to live in and I am here to say thank you to those who choose to stand with me even when it seems we stand alone, we are never alone because God always stands before us, beside us and within us and with that who can stand against us? as for me I live in the shelter of God's grace and mercy with all of my faith and trust.

I come before my God in my most humble gratitude for his generous blessings of abundant proportions always blessing me beyond my expectations and beyond my needs that I may continue to give beyond my means with a most joyous heart. I am grateful for the intangible because these are the gifts that live within our core to share in generous proportion as God so generously blesses each of us with, he gives to each of us unique and bountiful blessings and father I am on bended knee standing taller than ever when I am kneeled before you in my most sincere prayer of ample gratitude beyond words and while I will never find mere words in all of the dictionaries in all of this world what I can do is show you everyday through my gracious actions. Thank you most of all for sacrificing your most sweet son to shed his innocent blood of absolution for our redemption to flow through our undeserving veins that we may find gratitude and live in abundance because of your forgiveness through the everlasting love of Jesus Christ and the power of the Holy Ghost, embraced in your amazing grace. I commit to living through the soul of a child seeing this world through the innocent eyes of a child with all of my faith, trust and belief. I love you. Amen.
~Lisa

Father in heaven above as I look up I see your face, I stand tallest kneeled before you in my humble gratitude of the blessings you continue to place before me each and everyday in abundant proportion far exceeding my expectations and father because of your strength I stand even when I stand alone, because of your grace I am saved and thrive in the warmth of your embrace, because of your mercy I forgive the inexcusable because you have forgiven the inexcusable in each of us, and father I pray through my actions and my voice to touch one heart with your love, to move one soul with your mercy, and to inspire one life with your grace. Father I am faithfully yours, I am grateful for my life, for the gift of living my life through the eyes of a child while trusting everyone with the innocence of an infant in the arms of sweet amazing grace. Father thank you for sacrificing your sweet son Jesus Christ to shed his powerful blood of redemption through our veins that we may live in absolute gratitude and have everlasting life, I have faith, trust, and I believe with everything that is me in you. Amen.
~Lisa Christiansen

Ephesians 2: 8-10
8 For it is by grace you have been saved, through faith and this is not from yourselves, it is the gift of God 9 not by works, so that no one can boast. 10 For we are God's handiwork, created in Christ Jesus to do good works, which God prepared in advance for us to do.

It is said that you can't change the world, I believe you can change the facts and when you change the facts you change points of view, if you change points of view you might change a vote and when you change a vote you might change the world... You can't change who you are but you can change how you think, once you change how you think you will change what you believe and when you change what you believe you change who you are and become a new you... A new year is upon us and a new you is ready to be born...

What 11 Things Are You? These 11 Things Make Me Who I am.
1. I feel most alive on my bicycle.
2. I am always grateful
3. I know there is a reason for everything
4. I always look for the opportunity in everything
5. I appreciate life even when things seem overwhelming because I am learning ways to serve others through this experience.
6. I am only here to impress God and myself through serving others.
7. I love to buy a meal for the "lonely" in a restaurant anonymously.
8. I love to treat the car behind me to Starbucks even though I don't know who they are.
9. I love to give money to the people on the street because they are God's angels testing our inner faith and compassion.
10. I love to hug people because I can feel their true character through their touch.
11. I love to tell people "I love you" because I need to know that they feel they matter to me and because their love matters to me. There is no greater compliment than to earn the love of others with nothing required and I will be the difference I want to see in this world even if it means I stand alone.

It is said that you can't change the world, I believe you can change the facts and when you change the facts you change points of view, if you change points of view you might change a vote and when you change a vote you might change the world... You can't change who you are but you can change how you think, once you change how you think you will change what you believe and when you change what you believe you change who you are and become a new you... A new year is upon us and a new you is ready to be born...

Heavenly Father, This is Lisa Christiansen again, Your Warrior once again prepares for battle on behalf of those in need, your loyal and faithful servants, your favored children. Today I claim victory over Satan by putting on the whole Armor of God! I put on the Girdle of Truth! May I stand firm in the truth of your word so I will expose Satan's lies. I put on the breastplate of righteousness! May it guard my heart so I will remain pure and holy, protected under the blood of Jesus Christ. I put on the Shoes of Peace! May I stand firm in the good news of the gospel so your peace will shine through me and be a light to all I encounter. I take the shield of faith! I put on the Helmet of Salvation! May I keep my mind focused on you so because only then do I have control of my thoughts. I take the Sword of the Spirit! May the two-edged sword of Your word be ready in my hands so I can expose the tempting words of Satan. By faith I as your faithful warrior have put on the whole Armour of God! I am prepared to live this day in spiritual victory! As I come to you today in prayer through the love of Christ, the power of the Holy Ghost, and the authority of God our father that blessing be placed before you and you are prepared to see the opportunity and embrace it with passion. I pray for the genuine forgiveness that heals any hurts or wrongs. It strengthens the disheartened soul that has lost its way. It refreshes and renews our hope. It is through forgiveness that we are "born again" and "become like a child." In this way we regain the precious attitude of a willing mind that is ready to learn all over again as for me I am just a girl, a child of God who realizes that I fall short of Gods grace everyday and I recognize that God gives it to me out of his amazing grace. I am blessed each day that I awake and choose to share it with all of God's children, each of you. Thank you father for blessing me with what I don't deserve and protecting me from what I do deserve. I am enough for God and that's enough for me, I have placed my eyes upon him and found the truth in God's word. I pray that we each allow God to soften our soul to forgive completely, give gratitude infinitely and find our eyes upon him because only then will we see... Amen
~Lisa Christiansen

I pray that we see the gifts placed before us, I thank you authentically for coming into my life for a moment in time, for a lifetime, and for eternity. I freely pray for each of you love, health and wealth in abundance through Gods amazing grace. I pray that the enemy is freed from the chains that bind in the bondage of anger and pain to the loving innocence that they may experience life through the eyes of a child and father thank you for the beautiful, precious gift of seeing life in all of it's glory through the innocent eyes of a child that we may always see the beauty through the darkness as we light the way for others Father thank you for blessing me so abundantly with your grace, I am humbled deeply with gratitude for your everlasting love that you give so freely, thank you for sacrificing your only son Jesus Christ to shed his blood of redemption through our veins flooding our souls with forgiveness so we may live in gratitude. Thank you for the blessings you continue to place before me each and everyday, thank you for the unique gifts of still seeing this world through the eyes of a child with the faith of the innocence of the child that lives within me. Thank you for trusting me with your blessings to share among those in need, thank you for keeping me in your hands of safety as you use me as your vessel to reach out to others sharing your love through your word. Father thank you for bringing me into this world as your child, Father, give me strength, Lord, so when I speak, my words reach and inspire somebody, Lord, when they see me, let them see you. When they hear me, Father, let them hear you. Father God I know you abide by me and I abide by you today and everyday. I invite you God to live in me so when I step out, I'm representing the God I serve, I'm representing the family who loved me and those who cared for me as blessings in their challenge. Father I pray forgiveness for those who passed without accepting Christ that they may be welcomed in God's embrace and gratitude for God accepting all lost souls even if this means I must take their place, I pray they each know God's everlasting love, amazing infinite grace through the strength of the Holy Ghost, in Jesus name, Amen.

Today I would like everyone to take a self inventory of your life and search for new ways to be a pleasure in the sight of God today, remember those in need are Angels among us, Jesus in disguise waiting to see what we will do. To each person today has a different significance to me today is returning to the foundation, the core, the beginning of remembering Christ who died on the cross so that we may continue to live in gratitude and forgiveness. I believe that we are one nation under God and to me one nation under God is not exclusive to the United States of America, one nation under God means we are all of Gods children, this entire world.

So I will close with this quote, this scripture, and this prayer for all of us.

1. "We stand together as we did two centuries One people under God determined that our future shall be worthy of our past." ~President Ronald Reagan, Jan. 21, 1985
2. Lamentations 5:21 Restore us to yourself, Lord, that we may return; renew our days as of old.
3. Today my prayer is gratitude for all, I am most grateful to wake in Gods glory with angels among us to lift each other in prayer with only gratitude for the abundant blessings that God continues to place before each of us every moment with each breath we take and the wisdom to recognize these opportunities. Above all else gratitude for sacrificing your son to shed his blood of forgiveness through our veins that we may continue to live in gratitude and forgiveness. In Jesus holy name with the almighty power of the Holy Ghost and Gods everlasting love and infinite grace. Amen.
~Lisa Christiansen

Most precious father in heaven above I come before you humbled on bended knee in prayer to thank you for waking me up in your glory and grace filled with abundant mercy and generous gifts of opportunities of blessings beyond measure in abundant proportion, overwhelming me with gifts beyond my needs that I may continue to give beyond my means. I am grateful with a joyous soul for the great portions of gifts you continue to place before me each and everyday. Thank you for my life filled with your sweet son Christ Jesus, my heart filled with peace, my soul filled with love and for your glorious word, thank you for bringing these beautiful people and opportunities into my life that I may share my life as your vessel that others may hear me in a way that they hear your voice in my words and see you in my actions. Father thank you for always walking beside me, before me and within me filling my soul with your everlasting love. Thank you for being my shelter of love, my strength through my weakness, and my power through your word as I come before you to thank you for placing food in the stomachs of the hungry, feeding the thirsty, quenching the souls of the homeless and helpless with the warmth and comfort of your love. Thank you for blessing me with a heart of trust, thank you for blessing me with the trust of an infant and the soul of a child filled with unfiltered innocent trust to see others through the eyes of Jesus Christ that I may always be a pleasure in your eyes as I continue to search for new ways everyday to be a pleasure in your eyes to offer gratitude for your willingness to continue to protect me from everything I do deserve everyday and for the miracle of blessing me with more than I could ever earn or deserve. I thank you most of all for sacrificing your sweet son Jesus Christ to flood his powerful, innocent blood of absolution and redemption to flow through our veins that we may have everlasting life and have it more abundantly than we could ever earn or deserve. Father I confess with my mouth that Jesus Christ is my Lord and Savior, king of kings and I am committed to forever singing his praise for as long as I have breath and for as long as I have life I will share your word. Father thank you for always listening to my prayers and for your continued blessings, thank you for accepting those who have passed without accepting Christ that they may experience your glorious grace and mercy as they experience an eternal life in your kingdom even if this means I must take their place. I pray all of these things in Jesus Christ's holy name with the power of the Holy Ghost, the everlasting love of Jesus Christ embraced in your merciful grace, I have faith, trust, and I believe. Amen.
~Lisa Christiansen

Father I come before you tonight with a joyous heart filled with the faith of a child and with the trust of an infant. Thank you Father for blessing me with each passing moment beyond measure in abundant proportion, truly I am humbled in my gratitude as I come before you on bended knee standing taller than ever as I kneel before you in immeasurable gratitude for your amazing grace and mercy as you flood my soul with your faithful and unfailing love. Father thank you for standing beside me, before me and within me to use my weakness as your strength. Thank you for the gift of seeing this world through the eyes of a child, thank you for the gift of a heart of a child with blind trust to believe see the best in everyone, thank you for the opportunities placed before me each day and the ability to recognize the opportunity to be a blessing to others, father I am grateful and honored to sing your praises each day because for as long as I have breath and as long as I have life I commit to singing your praise, sharing your word and living in gratitude. Thank you father for sacrificing your son Jesus Christ to shed his innocent blood of absolution for our redemption to flood through our veins to wash away our sins that we may always remember to live in gratitude for the forgiveness you have given us through your amazing grace and mercy. Father thank you for blessing those who have passed without accepting Jesus christ with your forgiveness that they may experience your kingdom even if this means I must take their place, I will stand even if this means I stand alone because I know I have been born into sin and I was selfish in my youth, there are not words to express me gratitude for your blessing me with more than I could ever earn or deserve and you continue protect me beyond what I could earn or deserve and for this I can show you through my actions by standing tall kneeled before you always. I love you father, I have faith, trust, and I believe in your faithful unfailing love. I say mountain move and so it is done. Amen.

Isaiah 55:11 so is my word that goes out from my mouth: It will not return to me empty, but will accomplish what I desire and achieve the purpose for which I sent it.

Forgiveness bears the fruit of life, vengeance breeds disapproval and destruction of all. Every year I see postings that say "let us not forget 9/11" referencing the attack of that day, what I would like to ask you is to remember the loved ones and their families because if we lose sight of the loved ones we never heal. We cannot hold an entire country responsible for those that brought this wound, by doing so we are creating our own environment of pain and those responsible win. Only forgiveness will set you free, to live in gratitude one must forgive completely, to forgive one must live in gratitude, only then will success show up beyond your expectations without limits allowing you to live the life and freedom. Freedom is not free it is a gift from God that we could never on or deserve, a debt that we could never repay.

On this day let us all remember that Forgiveness is greater than vengeance, compassion more powerful than Anger and although we cannot comprehend the infinite love of our creator, we can express it to one another, moment-by-moment, action-by-action to remind us of that love that will one day embrace us into eternity...

God's grace is always providing me with what I don't deserve, God's mercy is always protecting me from what I do deserve. I am just a girl, a child of God and I fall short of God's amazing grace everyday and recognize he gives it to me anyway and for this I am grateful.

"So is my word that goes out from my mouth: It will not return to me empty, but will accomplish what I desire and achieve the purpose for which I sent it." (Isaiah 55:11)

Proverbs:17 Do not gloat when your enemy falls; when he stumbles, do not let your heart rejoice, 18 or the LORD will see and disapprove and turn his wrath away from him... Something to remember...

 I believe that it is important that we forgive everything that happened that day because Christ died on the cross to teach us how to live in forgiveness and it is forgiveness that will set you free, when you forgive gratitude shows up in ways that you never imagined and when you choose to forgive that is when life is truly extraordinary, outstanding, and infinite. Today I choose to forgive because I know God already has. Each of us every day are embraced in God's grace and for those who are curious grace means forgiveness. I forgive anything, everything, and everyone.
~Lisa Christiansen

8) Be sober, be vigilant; because your adversary the devil walks about like a roaring lion, seeking whom he may devour. 9) Resist him, steadfast in the faith, knowing that the same sufferings are experienced by your brotherhood in the world. 10) But may the God of all grace, who called us to His eternal glory by Christ Jesus, after you have suffered a while, perfect, establish, strengthen, and settle you. 11) To Him be the glory and the dominion forever and ever. Amen.

1 peter 8-11
This references the will of satan to close our hearts and burden our souls in bondage to hatred... forgive and be free...

Everyday is such a blessing and I am once again humbled before my God on bended knee for the amazing, abundant blessings of immeasurable proportion placed before me, I am thankful beyond words for God's willingness to bless me beyond my needs that I may continue to give from a joyous heart beyond my means. I know that greater is he who is within us than he who is in the world, I am just a girl, a child of God, a peaceful warrior to share Gods word as he stands before me, beside me and within me to surrender fully as I continue to search for new ways to be a pleasure in the sight of God because I fall short of God's grace everyday and I recognize he gives it to me anyway out of his amazing grace. I thank our beautiful Lord and savior for his willingness to continue blessing me with what I could never earn or deserve as he continues to protect me from what I absolutely do deserve. Most of all I am brought to me knees in awesome wonder of God's gracious, unselfish gift of sacrificing his one and only precious son to shed his innocent and most powerful blood of redemption to flood our veins with his forgiveness that we may find gratitude in the intangibles, in everything and everyone because truly this is a debt I could never repay, the gift of everlasting life in immeasurable abundance. I am touched by the outpouring of opportunities as I look forward to fulfilling each of these gracious gifts. I am refreshed with a renewed, fervent passion to confess with my mouth that Jesus Christ is absolutely my Lord and Savior, King of Kings and I will sing his praises for as long as I have breath and for as long as I have life. I will forever put on the full armor of God to serve and surrender, to share his word and his grace in every opportunity that he has brought to me and continues to bring into my life. Thank you father for your amazing grace, your everlasting love and your sweet mercy. I love you, I have faith, I trust in Jesus, and I absolutely believe. Amen.
~Lisa Christiansen

The depth of gratitude that I have brings me before our Lord Jesus on bended knee in prayer for the many blessings placed behind me from years gone by, the abundant blessings placed before me in this very moment, and the infinite blessings placed within me for what is yet to come.

Isaiah 55:11
So shall my word be that goeth forth out of my mouth: it shall not return unto me void, but it shall accomplish that which I please, and it shall prosper in the thing whereto I sent it.

Thank you for the blessings you continue to place before me each and everyday, thank you for the unique gifts of still seeing this world through the eyes of a child with the faith of the innocence of the child that lives within me. Thank you for trusting me with your blessings to share among those in need, thank you for keeping me in your hands of safety as you use me as your vessel to reach out to others sharing your love through your word. Thank you for protecting each of us from what we clearly deserve and blessing us with what we could never earn or deserve. Thank you for always providing me the ability to give beyond my means so that you continue to bless me beyond my needs that I may share abundantly with others. Father thank you for bringing me into this world as your child, Father, give me strength, Lord, so when I speak, my words reach and inspire somebody, Lord, when they see me, let them see you. When they hear me, Father, let them hear you. Father God I know you abide by me and I abide by you today and everyday. I invite you God to live in me today for infinity so when I step out, I'm representing the God I serve, I'm representing the family who loved me and those who cared for me as blessings in their challenge. Father I pray forgiveness for those who passed without accepting Christ that they may be welcomed in God's embrace and gratitude for God accepting all lost souls even if this means I must take their place, I pray father God they each know your amazing grace, the everlasting love of your son Jesus Christ, and the power of the Holy Ghost, in Jesus name I give gratitude. Amen.

~Lisa Christiansen

Matthew 18:3-6
3 And he said: "Truly I tell you, unless you change and become like little children, you will never enter the kingdom of heaven. 4 Therefore, whoever takes the lowly position of this child is the greatest in the kingdom of heaven. 5 And whoever welcomes one such child in my name welcomes me.

On the dawn of this new day once again I have been reminded once again of my abundant blessings hidden in the actions of others, my beautiful aunt who simply didn't know how to say the words "I love you" showed me in every action of her enduring love and for this I am grateful. My father "Papa" gave me an act of love that lives today in his wisdom, lessons of faith, always teaching me that God gives immeasurably in abundant proportion to those who give beyond their means. My mother who never wanted children gave me the gift of love through her last words reminding me to always keep my strength through God by boasting in my weakness and submitting to be God's vessel through remaining humble in vulnerability and the only way to accomplish this is to remain a child. Jessica and Patches have taught me to be grateful because your biggest problem is someone else's greatest blessing, my life is a blessing because of the sacrifice my God has given through sacrificing his beautiful baby boy Jesus Christ to shed his blood of redemption and absolution through our undeserving veins that we may have everlasting life and have it more abundantly flooding our life with abundant blessings in immeasurable proportion reminding us to always give beyond our means because he always gives beyond our needs. I am in love with my God, my Lord and Savior, King of Kings who rescued me as his daughter to share his word and as I confess with my mouth and shout to the world as I softly sing his praises as long as I have breath and for as long as I have life I will speak his name in gratitude humbled on bended knee because it is then that I stand tallest in his glorious amazing grace. My savior loves, my savior lives, my savior's always there for me, my God he has always been, my God he is, my God he will always be, I am just a girl, a child of God who realizes I fall short of God's amazing grace everyday and I recognize he gives it to me anyway because of his unfailing love, his faithful promise to each of us, because I have immeasurable faith, infinite trust, and I believe with all that I am. I pray all of this gratitude in Jesus Christ most holy name on high. Amen.
~Lisa Christiansen

WOW... My God proves his faithful unfailing love everyday and today is better than everyday before and just when I think it can't get any better it does, thank you father God for again blessing me in immeasurable proportion of abundance beyond my needs that I may give beyond my means. For as long as I have breath, for as long as my heart beats I will praise your holy name father in heaven. Today I come before you to join me in prayer, Father thank you for blessing me so abundantly in your grace, for embracing me in your faithful and everlasting love. Thank you for the blessings you continue to place before me so abundantly, thank you for opening my heart to recognize the blessings within the opportunities. Thank you for accepting my soul as a work in progress always shaping and molding me into your design. Thank you for always believing in me, thank you for strengthening me through vulnerability to breakthrough the chains of bondage we know as our imperfections to breakthrough to live by example rather than to lead by ignorance. Thank you for always protecting me from what I absolutely deserve and for blessing me with what I could never earn or deserve, for everything in my life is God's perfect design as my every decision is of God, by God and for God first, last and always. I pray gratitude for blessing everyone on their journey with protection, prosperity and well being. I thank you for that each of us are chosen for a unique purpose to share God's word of love, life, and fulfillment. I pray this in the name of Jesus Christ as I thank you most of all for sacrificing your only son to shed his blood of forgiveness through our veins that we may live in gratitude as forgiveness is the debt he paid that we may know freedom and everlasting life, a debt we can never repay. I pray father forgive them for they know not what they do, please have mercy on the souls that have passed without accepting Christ that they may be received and welcomed into heaven even if this means I take their place. Thank you for the courage to stand even if it means I stand alone, I pray gratitude for God's grace with the power vested in me through the Holy Ghost, through the everlasting love of Christ embraced in God's blessing and amazing grace, I am deeply humbled in gratitude, fueled by faith driven by God. Amen.
~Lisa Christiansen
Matthew 5:43-48

Most precious father in heaven above I come before you humbled on bended knee in prayer to thank you for waking me up in your glory and grace filled with abundant mercy and generous gifts of opportunities of blessings beyond measure in abundant proportion, overwhelming me with gifts beyond my needs that I may continue to give beyond my means. I am grateful with a joyous soul for the great portions of gifts you continue to place before me each and everyday. Thank you for my life filled with your sweet son Christ Jesus, my heart filled with peace, my soul filled with love and for your glorious word, thank you for bringing these beautiful people and opportunities into my life that I may share my life as your vessel that others may hear me in a way that they hear your voice in my words and see you in my actions. Father thank you for always walking beside me, before me and within me filling my soul with your everlasting love. Thank you for being my shelter of love, my strength through my weakness, and my power through your word as I come before you to thank you for placing food in the stomachs of the hungry, feeding the thirsty, quenching the souls of the homeless and helpless with the warmth and comfort of your love. Thank you for blessing me with a heart of trust, thank you for blessing me with the trust of an infant and the soul of a child filled with unfiltered innocent trust to see others through the eyes of Jesus Christ that I may always be a pleasure in your eyes as I continue to search for new ways everyday to be a pleasure in your eyes to offer gratitude for your willingness to continue to protect me from everything I do deserve everyday and for the miracle of blessing me with more than I could ever earn or deserve. I thank you most of all for sacrificing your sweet son Jesus Christ to flood his powerful, innocent blood of absolution and redemption to flow through our veins that we may have everlasting life and have it more abundantly than we could ever earn or deserve. Father I confess with my mouth that Jesus Christ is my Lord and Savior, king of kings and I am committed to forever singing his praise for as long as I have breath and for as long as I have life I will share your word. Father thank you for always listening to my prayers and for your continued blessings, thank you for accepting those who have passed without accepting Christ that they may experience your glorious grace and mercy as they experience an eternal life in your kingdom even if this means I must take their place. I pray all of these things in Jesus Christ's holy name with the power of the Holy Ghost, the everlasting love of Jesus Christ embraced in your merciful grace, I have faith, trust, and I believe. Amen. ~Lisa Christiansen

I wish you a most abundant new year with health and prosperity with many more to follow. I pray in gratitude kneeled before our father God to always heal you and hold you as he is the great physician, I pray that he always keeps your heart warm with a smile on your face and peace in your soul. I pray that God will always be first last and always in every decision that comes before you, I pray that you always keep your eyes fixed up on him because as long as we have our eyes fixed on him we will always see. I pray that God always puts passion in your vision and vision in your passion, I pray that he nourishes your soul with the feast of his word, and I pray that he nourishes your body with the healing power of the Holy Ghost. I pray that he fills your heart with love and your soul with a joy that is ever growing, and I thank him for bringing us to into each others lives and creating a bond that is completely of God, by God, and for God. I pray that he has mercy on the souls of the lost, I pray that he welcomes each and everyone of them into his kingdom to enjoy his peace, I pray that he excepts those that have not excepted Christ even if this means I must take their place. I pray all of these things in Jesus name and in his name sake, amen.

I love you my dear family In Christ, I am so proud of you and I'm grateful for you. I appreciate this gift given to me from our father God.
~Lisa Christiansen

Patches, I sit in humble gratitude for your love, for Jessica and the day I wasn't going to stop in that little town in the middle of somewhere on my way to nowhere on some something ride "Freewheel" my first cross state ride with abuse hidden . God had other plans for me as he brought me into your family before I ever knew what happened this little girl from Tahlequah with no "blood" relatives inherited God's continued blessings of grace that no man deserves through your love, the love of his most powerful angels of strength. Many days I stand in awe of awesome wonder of his miraculous works and how he brings such peace in the beauty of you. I have many times prayed not to ask for a single thing, I pray to say thank you for the precious gift of you, Jessica and the rest of our beautiful family. I love each of you more than you could possibly ever know and words will never convey the depth of respect I have for you. I have a love for you that exceeds love of myself, nothing required, I need no permission and no validation. I need no recognition and no reward, I simply most extraordinarily love you!

~Lisa

I come to you today in prayer through the love of Christ, the power of the Holy Ghost, and the authority of God our father that blessing be placed before you and should they be disguised as challenges you are prepared to see the opportunity and embrace it with passion. I pray for the genuine forgiveness that heals any hurts or wrongs. It strengthens the disheartened soul that has lost its way. It refreshes and renews our hope. It is through forgiveness that we are "born again" and "become like a child." In this way we regain the precious attitude of a willing mind that is ready to learn all over again as for me I am just a girl, a child of God who realizes that I fall short of Gods grace everyday and I recognize that God gives it to me out of his amazing grace. I am blessed each day that I awake and choose to share it with all of God's children. Thank you father for blessing me with what I don't deserve and protecting me from what I do deserve. I am enough for God and that's enough for me, I have placed my eyes upon him and found the truth in God's word. I pray that you also allow God to soften your soul to forgive completely, give gratitude infinitely and find your eyes upon him because only then will you see... I pray that you see the gifts placed before you, I thank you authentically for coming into my life for a moment in time, for a lifetime, and for eternity. I freely pray for you love, health and wealth in abundance through Gods grace... Amen
~Lisa Christiansen

Father in heaven above I pray on bended knee my deepest gratitude for all of the blessings that you have bestowed upon each one of us so abundantly, I pray that I have given you ample gratitude for the blessings that you continue to place in my life with opportunities I once only dreamed of, I come before you in prayer as a child of God for each of your children to prosper in your word as I continue to boast in my weakness because you are my strength. I love you and I thank you for giving me this beautiful day to rejoice in you as I praise you with the heart of a child through faith born from the womb of your ever-growing love and grace from the size of a mustard seed and flourishing daily like the mighty bamboo. Thank you father for closing my eyes like an infant that I may see you like the newborn feels its mother. Father, give me strength, Lord, so when I speak, my words reach and inspire somebody, My God, when they see me, let them see you. When they hear me, Father, let them hear you. Father God I know you abide by me and I abide by you today and everyday. I invite you God to live in me today for infinity so when I step out, I'm representing the God I serve, I'm representing the family who loved me and those who cared for me as blessings in their challenge. Father I pray forgiveness for those who passed without accepting Christ that they may be welcomed in God's embrace and gratitude for God accepting all lost souls even if this means I must take their place, I pray father God they each know your amazing grace, the everlasting love of your son Jesus Christ, and the power of the Holy Ghost, in Jesus name I give gratitude. Amen. ~Lisa Christiansen

Thank you for the blessings you continue to place before me each and everyday, thank you for the unique gifts of still seeing this world through the eyes of a child with the faith of the innocence of the child that lives within me. Thank you for trusting me with your blessings to share among those in need, thank you for keeping me in your hands of safety as you use me as your vessel to reach out to others sharing your love through your word. Thank you for protecting each of us from what we clearly deserve and blessing us with what we could never earn or deserve. Thank you for always providing me the ability to give beyond my means so that you continue to bless me beyond my needs that I may share abundantly with others.

Father thank you for bringing me into this world as your child, Father, give me strength, Lord, so when I speak, my words reach and inspire somebody, Lord, when they see me, let them see you. When they hear me, Father, let them hear you. Father God I know you abide by me and I abide by you today and everyday. I invite you God to live in me today for infinity so when I step out, I'm representing the God I serve, I'm representing the family who loved me and those who cared for me as blessings in their challenge. Father I pray forgiveness for those who passed without accepting Christ that they may be welcomed in God's embrace and gratitude for God accepting all lost souls even if this means I must take their place, I pray father God they each know your amazing grace, the everlasting love of your son Jesus Christ, and the power of the Holy Ghost, in Jesus name I give gratitude. Amen.
~Lisa Christiansen

Matthew 18:3-6
3 And he said: "Truly I tell you, unless you change and become like little children, you will never enter the kingdom of heaven. 4 Therefore, whoever takes the lowly position of this child is the greatest in the kingdom of heaven. 5 And whoever welcomes one such child in my name welcomes me.

Father in heaven above I pray on bended knee my deepest gratitude for all of the blessings that you have bestowed upon each one of us so abundantly, I pray that I have given you ample gratitude for the blessings that you continue to place in my life with opportunities I once only dreamed of, I come before you in prayer as a child of God for each of your children to prosper in your word as I continue to boast in my weakness because you are my strength. I love you and I thank you for giving me this beautiful day to rejoice in you as I praise you with the heart of a child through faith born from the womb of your ever-growing love and grace from the size of a mustard seed and flourishing daily like the mighty bamboo. Thank you father for closing my eyes like an infant that I may see you like the newborn feels its mother. Father, give me strength, Lord, so when I speak, my words reach and inspire somebody, My God, when they see me, let them see you. When they hear me, Father, let them hear you. Father God I know you abide by me and I abide by you today and everyday. I invite you God to live in me today for infinity so when I step out, I'm representing the God I serve, I'm representing the family who loved me and those who cared for me as blessings in their challenge. Father I pray forgiveness for those who passed without accepting Christ that they may be welcomed in God's embrace and gratitude for God accepting all lost souls even if this means I must take their place, I pray father God they each know your amazing grace, the everlasting love of your son Jesus Christ, and the power of the Holy Ghost, in Jesus name I give gratitude. Amen.

The depth of gratitude I have for you is beyond words or understanding. Only God knows the definition of the magnitude of my appreciation for the day he intertwined our paths forever bonding us in the holy name of his only son Jesus Christ. I know that I am not the person I once was from the moment I met Jessica everything I thought I knew about my faith was redefined that day, my gratitude became alive in the smallest things that I now see as the big things and my level of forgiveness has become indescribable, I have learned to forgive the inexcusable because Christ forgives the inexcusable in each of us everyday and I remember a story when Jessica said "It's Ok, just pray, God forgave them already" and because of that I know how to forgive everything no matter what and for that I thank you because I now live in gratitude and forgiveness all because of Christ's example that he placed before me in his angel Jessica... I love you. I trust in Jesus!!!... Always and forever...

With All Of My Gratitude,

What a Beautiful and amazing day in God's grace... Everyday God is great and God is great everyday...

Thank you for the blessings you continue to place before me each and everyday, thank you for the unique gifts of still seeing this world through the eyes of a child with the faith of the innocence of the child that lives within me. Thank you for trusting me with your blessings to share among those in need, thank you for keeping me in your hands of safety as you use me as your vessel to reach out to others sharing your love through your word. Thank you for protecting each of us from what we clearly deserve and blessing us with what we could never earn or deserve. Thank you for always providing me the ability to give beyond my means so that you continue to bless me beyond my needs that I may share abundantly with others.

Father thank you for bringing me into this world as your child, Father, give me strength, Lord, so when I speak, my words reach and inspire somebody, Lord, when they see me, let them see you. When they hear me, Father, let them hear you. Father God I know you abide by me and I abide by you today and everyday. I invite you God to live in me today for infinity so when I step out, I'm representing the God I serve, I'm representing the family who loved me and those who cared for me as blessings in their challenge. Father I pray forgiveness for those who passed without accepting Christ that they may be welcomed in God's embrace and gratitude for God accepting all lost souls even if this means I must take their place, I pray father God they each know your amazing grace, the everlasting love of your son Jesus Christ, and the power of the Holy Ghost, in Jesus name I give gratitude. Amen.

~Lisa Christiansen

Matthew 18:3-6

3 And he said: "Truly I tell you, unless you change and become like little children, you will never enter the kingdom of heaven. 4 Therefore, whoever takes the lowly position of this child is the greatest in the kingdom of heaven. 5 And whoever welcomes one such child in my name welcomes me.

Let us come together as one,

The Bible says the prayer of a righteous person is powerful and effective, yet something extraordinary happens when two or more agree together in prayer. In Matt. 18:19, Jesus said, "If any two of you agree touching any matter on this earth, it shall be done."

Write your Prayer and the world will be praying for you and your cause.

Forgiveness is greater than vengeance, compassion more powerful than Anger...
Today I choose to write about forgiveness because Christ has chosen this as his example for us to follow and I would rather follow a great example than to lead by ignorance.

Forgiveness is a promise to take control of your feelings because when you forgive others you are making a commitment to release the past, live in the present and receive the gift of life through Jesus Christ.

Take a moment to pray for the strength to release those who have wronged you into God's grace so that he may bless you with everlasting life.
Forgiveness is both a decision and a real change in emotional experience. That change is related to and a direct result of better mental health and physical wealth.

Find your peace because life is short, if asked when will you die the answer is so simple that it's complicated... "in one breath" Life ends with a breath and death begins with a breath... live like today like it is your last because somebody took your place today, make them proud...

I believe that we must go where we are needed as did Christ not making ourselves exclusive to the righteous, we must embrace non-believers and believers equally with the word of God as we share the everlasting love of Jesus Christ through the gift of the Holy Ghost as we are commanded by God to keep our eyes upon him. I appreciate your prayers and will return the favor by praying for our Holy Father to soften our hearts and open our soul to submit to God's will completely. I pray for our spirit to be freed from the chains of bondage so our childlike innocence may once again shine bright and allow each of us to breakthrough to the freedom of loving all of God's Children equally. I pray for each of you a life filled with a happiness born from the womb of joy, love born from Gods design, and health born from the healing hands of Christ's blood shed to flow through our veins offering gratitude embraced in the Holy Spirit. I pray this in gratitude for the blessings that I am so abundantly gifted with, I am grateful for the blessings placed before me today and everyday as I continue to find strength in faith through the power of the Holy Ghost, the love of Christ while embraced in Gods infinite grace. I pray for the lost to find their way and for God's mercy to rest upon those that have passed without accepting Christ for their salvation that they may be spared and given a home in heaven even if it means my soul must take their place... Amen ~Lisa Christiansen

Thank you father for blessing me, thank you for showering me with your abundance and your grace. Thank you for sacrificing your son Jesus Christ on the cross to shed his blood of redemption through our veins that we may live in gratitude and forgiveness, thank you for blessing me with far more than I could ever earned or deserve and equally I thank you for protecting me from everything that I do deserve. Father I come before you on bended knee and humble gratitude for your mercy, thank you for the souls that have passed without accepting your son Jesus Christ that they are forgiven so they may enter into your kingdom even if this means I must take their place. Father thank you for giving me life, thank you for the gift of seeing this world through the eyes I have a child, thank you for blessing me with the gift of living my life with the soul of a child filled with laughter and joy and thank you for my heart that sees the best in everyone, forgives through your example and believes in you with unbridled passion. I pray all of these things in Jesus holy name. Amen

 I pray in gratitude kneeled before our father God to always heal you and hold, keep you and mold you as he is the great physician, I pray that he always keeps your heart warm with a smile on your face and peace in your soul. I pray that God will always be first last and always in every decision that comes before you, I pray that you always keep your eyes fixed up on him because as long as we have our eyes fixed on him we will always see. I pray that God always puts passion in your vision and vision in your passion, I pray that he nourishes your soul with the feast of his word, and I pray that he nourishes your body with the healing power of the Holy Ghost. I pray that he fills your heart with love and your soul with a joy that is ever growing, and I thank him for bringing us to into each others lives and creating a bond that is completely of God, by God, and for God. I pray that he has mercy on the souls of the lost, I pray that he welcomes each and everyone of them into his kingdom to enjoy his peace, I pray that he excepts those that have not excepted Christ even if this means I must take their place. I pray all of these things in Jesus name and in his name sake, Amen.

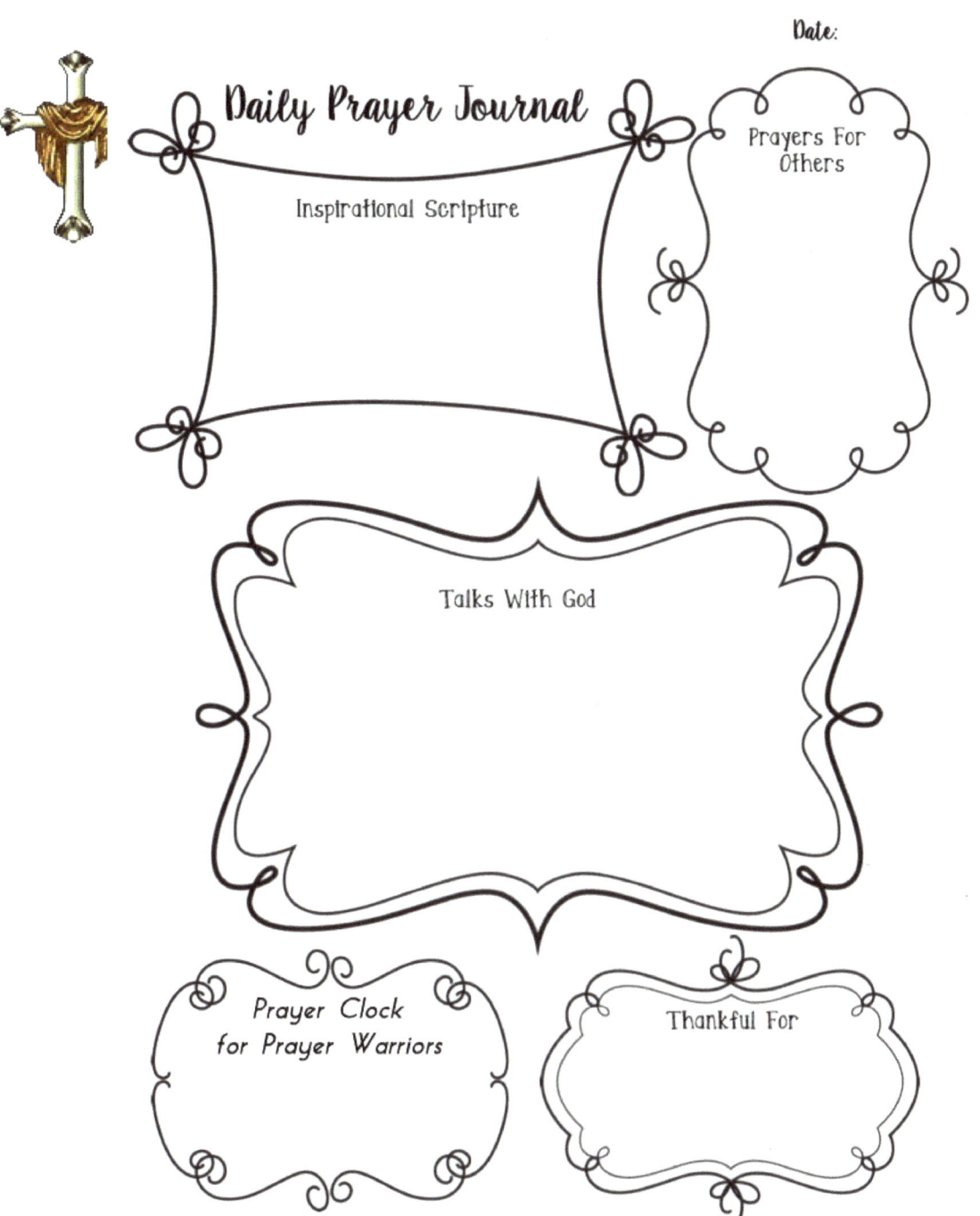

 Everyday I pray to God a thank you as I open my eyes... Ever since I was a child I prayed "Should I ever make it to my outcome I will continue to be grateful, should I ever be in a position of influence I will use it for the greater good of all,... Everyday I do whatever I can, however big or small, to make a difference in the world with the intention to touch the hearts of others, planting the seed of love, gratitude for even the intangible and forgiveness of the soul even if only one person is touched it is all worth it..." And I am grateful, thank you to God first, last and always. Thank you to each of you for your generous support through your authentic kindness as you each inspire me everyday...

As long as I have breath I will sing his praise, I will kneel to stand tall and I will pray without ceasing for the abundant blessings placed within me, upon me, before me and behind me by my father God, Jesus Christ and the Holy Ghost because I am grateful. Amen

~Lisa Christiansen

 I thank my God through my lord and savior Jesus Christ for abundantly blessing me beyond what I could ever earn or deserve and for protecting me from everything I most certainly deserve as I boast in my weakness for almighty God to shine his strength through me as I surrender myself to be the vessel of his message...

Father in heaven above I pray on bended knee my deepest gratitude for all of the blessings that you have bestowed upon each one of us so abundantly, I pray that I have given you ample gratitude for the blessings that you continue to place in my life with opportunities I once only dreamed of, I come before you in prayer as a child of God for each of your children to prosper in your word as I continue to boast in my weakness because you are my strength. I love you and I thank you for giving me this beautiful day to rejoice in you as I praise you with the heart of a child through faith born from the womb of your ever-growing love and grace from the size of a mustard seed and flourishing daily like the mighty bamboo. Thank you father for closing my eyes like an infant that I may see you like the newborn feels its mother. Father, give me strength, Lord, so when I speak, my words reach and inspire somebody, My God, when they see me, let them see you. When they hear me, Father, let them hear you. Father God I know you abide by me and I abide by you today and everyday. I invite you God to live in me today for infinity so when I step out, I'm representing the God I serve, I'm representing the family who loved me and those who cared for me as blessings in their challenge. Father I pray forgiveness for those who passed without accepting Christ that they may be welcomed in God's embrace and gratitude for God accepting all lost souls even if this means I must take their place, I pray father God they each know your amazing grace, the everlasting love of your son Jesus Christ, and the power of the Holy Ghost, in Jesus name I give gratitude. Amen.

I come to you tonight in prayer through the love of Christ, the power of the Holy Ghost, and the authority of God our father that blessing be placed before you and you are prepared to see the opportunity and embrace it with passion. Thank you for the blessings you continue to place before me each and everyday, thank you for the unique gifts of still seeing this world through the eyes of a child with the faith of the innocence of the child that lives within me. Thank you for trusting me with your blessings to share among those in need, thank you for keeping me in your hands of safety as you use me as your vessel to reach out to others sharing your love through your word. Thank you for protecting each of us from what we clearly deserve and blessing us with what we could never earn or deserve. Thank you for always providing me the ability to give beyond my means so that you continue to bless me beyond my needs that I may share abundantly with others.

Father thank you for bringing me into this world as your child, Father, give me strength, Lord, so when I speak, my words reach and inspire somebody, Lord, when they see me, let them see you. When they hear me, Father, let them hear you. Father God I know you abide by me and I abide by you today and everyday. I invite you God to live in me today for infinity so when I step out, I'm representing the God I serve, I'm representing the family who loved me and those who cared for me as blessings in their challenge. Father I pray forgiveness for those who passed without accepting Christ that they may be welcomed in God's embrace and gratitude for God accepting all lost souls even if this means I must take their place, I pray father God they each know your amazing grace, the everlasting love of your son Jesus Christ, and the power of the Holy Ghost, in Jesus name I give gratitude. Amen.

~Lisa Christiansen

What a beautiful day for remembering to live in forgiveness and gratitude, for these are the seeds that bear fruits of success beyond what your mind could ever conceive...

"I say to you, love your enemies, bless those who curse you, do good to those who hate you, and pray for those who spitefully use you and persecute you, that you may be sons and daughters of your Father in heaven."
(Matthew 5:44-46)

"Father, forgive them, for they know not what they do..."(Luke 23:34)

Let us all take a moment today to pray in our own way for each others success in health, wealth and happiness keeping the needs of others above our own will bring forth paychecks of the heart money cannot replace. What will you share for us to pray for?

I am just a girl, a child of God who realizes that I fall short of Gods grace everyday and I recognize that God gives it to me out of his amazing grace. I am blessed each day that I awake and choose to share it with all of God's children...

 Today I come before God in prayer for gratitude for the blessings he continues to place before me, I pray for the beautiful life he has blessed each of us with while bringing each of us into each others lives for reasons beyond our comprehension while infinitely his design, I pray Gratitude for God sacrificing his son Jesus Christ to die for our sins that we may be forgiven and in his name with the power of the Holy Ghost and Gods will. Amen

Forgiveness is greater than vengeance, compassion more powerful than Anger... Father forgive them for they know not what they do. This is who I choose to be everyday, I am not perfect. I walk everyday with these words so they always be my actions.

 Who will join me in this prayer tonight as I come before our heavenly father with the power of the holy ghost through the love of Jesus Christ I come in gratitude for the gifts and blessings placed before each of us everyday.

I pray thanks to our father for our loved ones to open their hearts and invite Jesus into their lives to free them from the chains that keep them in bondage and reveal the innocence to breakthrough and live free, most of all I come in gratitude for giving us the gift of sacrificing your son Jesus Christ to die for our sins and wash our souls in his holy blood offering us authentic, infinite and complete forgiveness.

I send all of you love and prosperity abundant in my prayers as they are filled with you to receive all of the best God has to offer, may you be blessed abundantly with good health, financial freedom, time wealth and a heart filled with love as you joyously celebrate the happiness of your fulfillment today and forever.
Amen

Ask God to OPEN YOUR EYES to see what is already in you (Ephesians 1:18, Ephesians 3:20). The Holy Spirit is in you. The Love of God is in you. Faith is in you. These forces of God's power are in you right now if you are born again.

Affirm this....I am complete in Christ. There is no good thing missing in my life. I have all things in Him. My God supplies all my needs, and I expect His supply TODAY. I have the peace of God, which delivers my heart from trouble and disappointment. Even if people let me down, my God will uphold me and help me. I have the Holy Spirit, the love of God and the gift of faith in my life. I am complete in Him, in Jesus' Name!

Thank you John Ramsey for this beautiful prayer.

~Lisa

I believe that we must go where we are needed as did Christ not making ourselves exclusive to the righteous, we must embrace non-believers and believers equally with the word of God as we share the everlasting love of Jesus Christ through the gift of the Holy Ghost as we are commanded by God to keep our eyes upon him. I appreciate your prayers and will return the favor by praying for our Holy Father to soften our hearts and open our soul to submit to God's will completely. I pray for our spirit to be freed from the chains of bondage so our childlike innocence may once again shine bright and allow each of us to breakthrough to the freedom of loving all of God's Children equally. I pray for each of you a life filled with a happiness born from the womb of joy, love born from Gods design, and health born from the healing hands of Christ's blood shed to flow through our veins offering gratitude embraced in the Holy Spirit. I pray this in gratitude for the blessings that I am so abundantly gifted with, I am grateful for the blessings placed before me today and everyday as I continue to find strength in faith through the power of the Holy Ghost, the love of Christ while embraced in Gods infinite grace. I pray for the lost to find their way and for God's mercy to rest upon those that have passed without accepting Christ for their salvation that they may be spared and given a home in heaven even if it means my soul must take their place… Amen

Daily Prayer Journal

Inspirational Scripture

Prayers For Others

Talks With God

Prayer Clock for Prayer Warriors

Thankful For

Lord's Prayer In Cherokee
ᎤᎬᏫᏳᎯ ᎤᏓᏙᎵᏍᏔᏅ Tugvwiyuhi udadolistanvi

ᎣᎩᏙᏓ ᎦᎸᏆᏗ ᎮᎯ,
ogidoda galvladi hehi
Our father heaven dweller,

ᎦᎸᏉᏗᏳ ᎨᏎᏍᏗ ᏕᏣᏙᎥᎢ.
galvquodiyu gesesdi detsadov'i
Glorified will be your name.

ᏣᎬᏫᏳᎯ ᎨᏒ ᏫᎦᎾᎾᎬᎢ,
tsagvwiyuhi gesv wigananugo'i
You are God let it be known,

ᎠᏂ ᎡᎶᎯ ᏫᏂᎦᎵᏍᏓ ᎭᏓᏅᏖᏍᎬᎢ.
ani elohi winigalisda hadanvtesgv'i
Here on earth let it be as you think it.

ᎾᏍᎩᏯ ᎦᎸᏆᏗ ᏥᏂᎦᎵᏍᏗᎭ.
nasgiya galvladi tsinigalisdiha
The same as in heaven it is done.

ᏂᏓᏙᏛᏇᏒ ᎣᎦᎵᏍᏓᏴᏗ ᏍᎩᏏ ᎪᎯ ᎢᎦ.
nidadodaquisv ogalisdayvdi sgivsi gohi iga
Everyday our food give it to us this day.

ᏗᎨᏍᎩᏴᏏᏉᏃ ᏕᏍᎩᏚᎬᎢ ᎾᏍᎩᏯ ᏥᏗᎦᏯᏲᏏᏁᎰ ᏦᏥᏚᎩ,
digesgi'vsiquono desgidugv'i nasgiya tsidigayotsineho tsotsidugi
Forgive us what we owe, like we forgive what others have done,
ᎠᎴ ᏞᏍᏗ ᎤᏓᎪᎵᏰᏗᏴ ᎨᏒ ᏫᏗᏍᎩᏯᏘᏅᏍᏔᏅᎩ,
ale tlesdi udagoliyediyi gesv widisgiyatinvstanvgi
And don't lead us to temptation,

ᏍᎩᏳᏓᎴᏍᎨᏍᏗᏉᏍᎩᏂ ᎤᏲ ᎨᏒᎢ.
sgiyudalesgesdiquosgini uyo gesv'i
But rescue us from evil.

ᏣᏤᎵᎦᏰᏃ ᏣᎬᏫᏳᎯ ᎨᏒᎢ,
tsatseligayeno tsagvwiyuhi gesv'i
Yours is the Kingdom,

ᎠᎴ ᏣᏛᎵᏂᎩᏗᏴ ᎨᏒᎢ.
ale tsahlinigidiyi gesv'i
And you are the strength,

ᎠᎴ ᎡᏣᎸᏉᏗᏳ ᎨᏒ ᏂᎪᎯᎸᎢ.
ale etsalvquodiyu gesv nigohilv'i
And your glory is forever.

ᎡᎺᏅ.
emenv
Amen.

I would rather follower a great example than lead by ignorance... I choose to have a relationship with God rather than have religion.

It's no secret that those of us who claim to follow Jesus Christ consistently fall short of the glory of God. Being a disciple of Jesus is a lifelong journey towards conforming ourselves to the image and way of life that Jesus taught. However, so often, followers of Jesus chose to blatantly ignore some of the clearest instruction of our teachers and obscure it with vague theology so that we can get off the hook. Other times, followers of Jesus are taught something explicitly contradictory to the plain words of Jesus and then spend their lives obeying the instruction they received instead of the commands of Jesus.

I was inspired to write this when someone dear to me once said this to me... "How can I honor the one who loves me so deeply when I display the character that I do for I am only human, how can I display any other character than I do when it is who I am, only God can change me for I cannot change myself as all I can do is choose to surrender to his grace and even surrender seems challenging sometimes and I realize it is through his amazing grace that will continue to carry me through to brighter tomorrows." I realize everyday I awake I fall short of God's grace, I also recognize God blesses me with his amazing grace each and everyday through his eternal love and everlasting life, this is why everyday I search for new ways to be a pleasure in the sight of God that he may continue to bless me and that he continues to use me as his vessel to bless others.

Remember the race is not won by the strong or the fast it is won by those who endure... Happiness is a state of mind, Joy lives in your heart through the amazing Grace of God flooding your soul with all the fuel you need to continue to have faith when others around you have lost all hope. It is then that you have the strength to share your faith with love...

EACH DAY IN SPORTS, LOVE AND LIFE I LIVE BY THESE PRINCIPLES; 1 Corinthians 9:24-27
24 Do you not know that in a race all the runners run, but only one gets the prize? Run in such a way as to get the prize. 25 Everyone who competes in the games goes into strict training. They do it to get a crown that will not last, but we do it to get a crown that will last forever. 26 Therefore I do not run like someone running aimlessly; I do not fight like a boxer beating the air. 27 No, I strike a blow to my body and make it my slave so that after I have preached to others, I myself will not be disqualified for the prize.

As we journey through life there can come times where we lose our way, this seldom comes as an abrupt change because it more often comes as a slow drift until one day we awaken to find ourselves far from the shore. A traveler who has lost his way needs one thing above all else a compass; God provides this to us through his word. God's word always points true north... Something to remember.

 I believe it is courage, heart and integrity that are one's true value because you cannot buy character, you cannot purchase courage and money won't buy happiness. These things are shaped by our own internal model of the world, our blueprint that shapes our morals, values and beliefs and our own compass. Every one of us, unconsciously, works out a personal philosophy of life, by which we are guided, inspired, and corrected, as time goes on. It is this philosophy by which we measure out our days, and by which we advertise to all about us the man, or woman, that we are. . . . It takes but a brief time to scent the life philosophy of anyone. It is defined in the conversation, in the look of the eye, and in the general mien of the person. It has no hiding place. It's like the perfume of the flower unseen, but known almost instantly. It is the possession of the successful, and the happy. And it can be greatly embellished by the absorption of ideas and experiences of the useful of this earth. Dreams pass into the reality of action. From the actions stems the dream again; and this interdependence produces the highest form of living. Most people can look back over the years and identify a time and place at which their lives changed significantly. Whether by accident or design, these are the moments when, because of a readiness within us and a collaboration with events occurring around us, we are forced to seriously reappraise ourselves and the conditions under which we live and to make certain choices that will affect the rest of our lives. Gratitude is the key to success, forgiveness is the key to gratitude... forgiveness will set you free...
~Lisa Christiansen

 I would always encourage people of any age not to be so quick to follow other people's truths but to search and follow your own moral code and live by your own integrity, and mostly just be brave.

If you don't have integrity, you have nothing. You can't buy it. You can have all the money in the world, but if you are not a moral and ethical person, you really have nothing.

No matter who you are or what your age do not be so quick to follow the values and beliefs of others you must search and follow your own moral code and live by your own integrity, be brave enough to step up. You do not need to stand tall you only need to stand up; God will take care of the rest.

I invite each of you to pray with me again this amazing evening... Dearest most precious Father in heaven above we come before you in humble adoration of the blessings you have placed before us today, for blessing us abundantly with nourishment to strengthen our faith, to feed our souls that we may share your word through our daily activities. Thank you for blessing me with the ability to ride strong as a testimonial to your great healing, thank you for giving me the gift of one of your most revered angels Jessica and blessing me with the family I have found in Patches, Thank you for the gift of sight to appreciate your most awesome art as I climb Mt. Scott and look out to the lake through the trees with the mountains so majestic, thank you for the gift of sound to hear the water fall so gently off of the mountain as I continue to climb, to hear the birds singing your praises, thank you for the gift just to breathe, to appreciate the ability to experience the gift of scent to smell the fragrance of the fresh flowers, the skunk that released it's aroma, the fresh pine aroma as I climb on my bicycle, Thank you for the gift of touch to feel the gift of the great pain that let's me know I am alive and blessed to participate in events and appreciate the ability to pedal each stroke as my thighs burn knowing that Jessica works so hard just to stand makes me appreciate each stroke of the gears and the ability to raise my hands in praise of your awesome grace that you give to each of us in our unique abilities and challenges teaching us there is no such thing as a disability rather the ability to inspire in your holy name. Thank you for the ability to taste, to share the beautiful flavors that Jessica fed me in the Bologna sandwich, Cheetos, Chocolate Chip Cookies and the Juice box that I so deeply appreciate, to experience the love of your greatness brings me to my knees in humble gratitude of your awesomeness, Thank you for that you sent your son from his home on high to pay a debt he did not owe for each of us as he shed his blood of forgiveness to flow through our veins that we may live in his example rather than to lead by ignorance. I pray gratitude that I am saved by your grace alone through the blood of Christ blessed by you father God on the highest with the power of the Holy Ghost. I pray gratitude that everyday you continue to gift me with the ability to live in gratitude through forgiveness. I pray for the souls that have passed without accepting Christ that you may have mercy on their souls and welcome them with open arms even if this means I must take their place, father I am committed to stand even if it means I stand alone because this is who you created me to be, Thank you for Christ teaching me to always ask "father forgive them for they know not what they do, thank you for my mother attempting to abort me because this taught me strength through vulnerability and thank you for my aunt not wanting me because this taught me that love is a gift you give without expectation of it's return. Thank you for the blessings you provided through my uncle and most of all thank you for sacrificing your son to save each and everyone of us and forgiving us as we are sinners in an imperfect word recognizing that the perfection is that this is your perfect design, always of God, by God and for God. Father God I love you my savior my God. Thank you. Amen

Everyday I see God's amazing grace all around me in everything, the breadth, depth and width of my humble authentic gratitude is immeasurable. Only God has the words for the level of appreciation I have for his amazing grace, his glorious willingness to continue to bless me in abundance of immeasurable proportion. Just when I think it can't get any better God steps in and shows my blessings beyond my expectation, thank you Lord Jesus Christ, King of Kings, my Savior my God for your favour of which I could never earn or deserve, for the debt of forgiveness through your shining son who shed his innocent blood of absolution and redemption to offer each of us everlasting life and to have it more abundantly, a debt we could never repay. Father I confess with my mouth that you are my lord and savior, king of kings, my God and I will forever sing your praises for as long as I have life I will share your word and for as long as I breath I will bear witness to your Glory, mercy and grace.

Father I will continue to search for new ways to be a pleasure in your sight, I will forever show gratitude for your blessing me beyond my needs by always giving beyond my means. Father I will always surrender to be your vessel to speak that others may hear you when I speak and see you through my every action, father, thank you for bringing me into this world as your child, Father, give me strength, Lord, so when I speak, my words reach and inspire somebody, Lord, when they see me, let them see you. When they hear me, Father, let them hear you. Father God I know you abide by me and I abide by you today and everyday. I invite you God to live in me today for infinity so when I step out, I'm representing the God I serve, I'm representing the family who loved me and those who cared for me as blessings in their challenge. Father I pray forgiveness for those who passed without accepting Christ that they may be welcomed in God's embrace and gratitude for God accepting all lost souls even if this means I must take their place, I pray father God they each know your amazing grace, the everlasting love of your son Jesus Christ, and the power of the Holy Ghost, in Jesus name I give gratitude. Amen.

~Lisa Christiansen

Father in heaven above I come before you on bended knee with humble gratitude I pray for this most beautiful angel among this, you're most revered most powerful warrior of prayer Jessica. Father in heaven above I want to thank you for Jessica and all of the prayers that she blesses upon me every day and every night and I want to thank you for the strength that she shows me, for the humility that she teaches me and for the love that you so abundantly bless me with through Jessica. Father in heaven above right now Jessica is weakened perfectly through your love because of the strength that she displays for others it has taken it's toll on her and father I come before you and ask of you with gratitude in advance for giving the physicians your hands, lending them your eyes and blessing them with your wisdom to heal her in your perfection. Father in heaven above I stand before you with my deepest gratitude for the day that I met Jessica, for that day changed my life forever, that was the day that you placed an angel among us in my life and allowed me to not only recognize it you gave me the ability to see it clearly with the most clarity that I've ever seen anything with and father I always pedal stronger when I think of Jessica, I pray harder when I feel her in my heart, I speak your word through Jessica's love and for that I truly want to thank you because I know that as we speak you are healing her you are removing obstacles and replacing them with abundance. I also want to thank you for Patches McAlister Mitchell, I want to thank you for showing me what beauty really is because The beauty that shines through patches to the surface is completely of God by God and for God she is a woman of integrity and strength, her beauty is in the way that she loves so selfless her strength is in the way that she accepts without condition, her power is in her vulnerability to live in your word and introduce others to your son Jesus Christ, father thank you so much for sacrificing your son on the cross to shed his blood of redemption through our veins that we may continue to live in gratitude and forgiveness and father I pray gratitude for bringing me into this world as your child, Father, give me strength, Lord, so when I speak, my words reach and inspire somebody, Lord, when they see me, let them see you. When they hear me, Father, let them hear you. My Dear God I know you abide by me and I abide by you today and everyday. I invite you God to live in me today for infinity so when I step out, I'm representing the God I serve, I'm representing the family who loved me and those who cared for me as blessings in their challenge. Father I pray forgiveness for those who passed without accepting Christ that they may be welcomed in God's embrace and gratitude for accepting all lost souls even if this means I must take their place, I pray father God they each know your amazing grace, the everlasting love of your son Jesus Christ, and the power of the Holy Ghost, in Jesus name I give gratitude. Amen. ~Lisa Christiansen

I LOVE YOU Jessica, I am truly blessed by riches that money cannot buy because God above places his angels among us at the doorways of my light to pray with innocent conviction, love without condition and live by his example through their every action... Jessica's love can be felt around the world but by no one more than I because of Patches gift of selfless sharing, complete love and full faith in our God above...

Matthew 18:2-6
2 He called a little child to him, and placed the child among them. 3 And he said: "Truly I tell you, unless you change and become like little children, you will never enter the kingdom of heaven. 4 Therefore, whoever takes the lowly position of this child is the greatest in the kingdom of heaven. 5 And whoever welcomes one such child in my name welcomes me.

~Lisa Christiansen

www.ingramcontent.com/pod-product-compliance
Lightning Source LLC
Chambersburg PA
CBHW040058160426
43192CB00003B/105